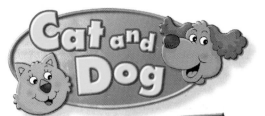

Go To School

By Nikki Chase   Illustrated by Mike Dammer

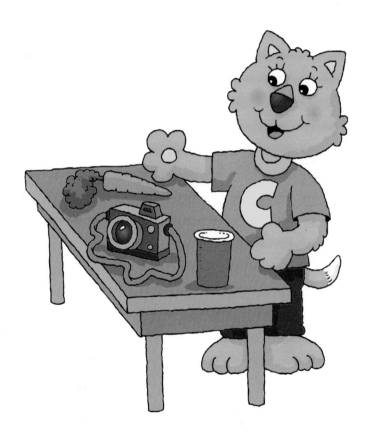

Target Skill Letter Recognition *Aa, Bb, Cc, Dd, Ee*
High-Frequency Words *I, am*

PEARSON

Scott
Foresman

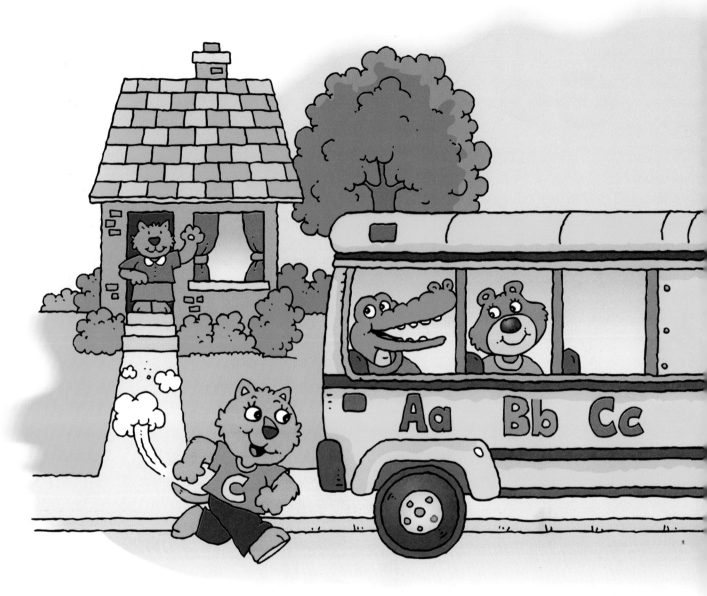

 I am Cat.

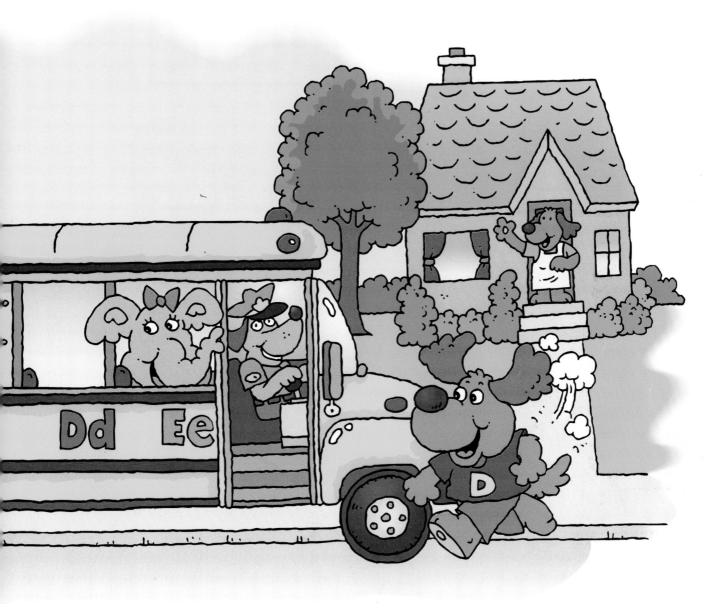

I am Dog.

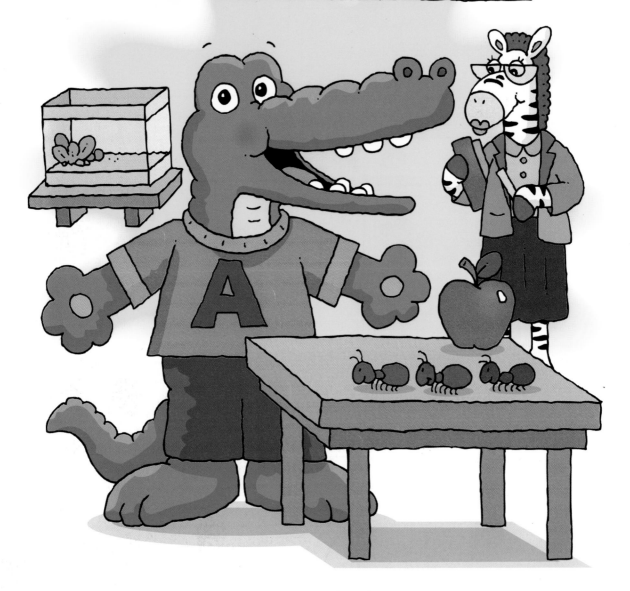

I am A.

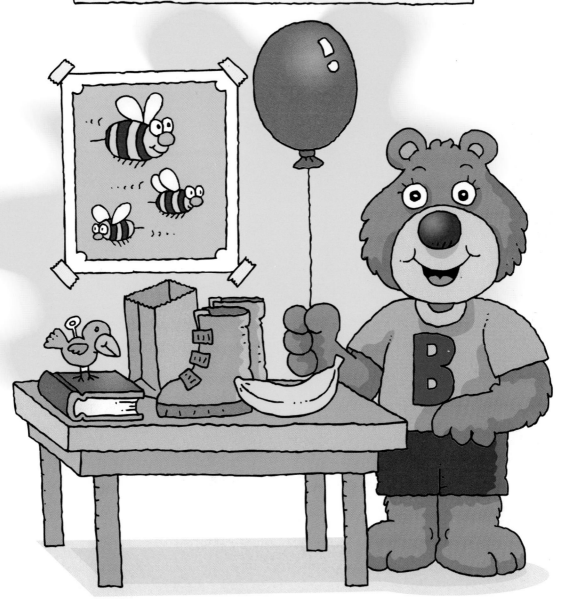

I am B.

AaBbCcDdEe

I am C.

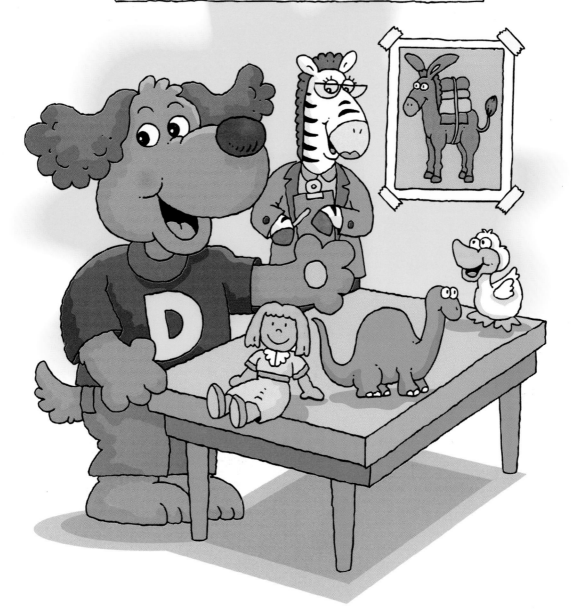

I am D.

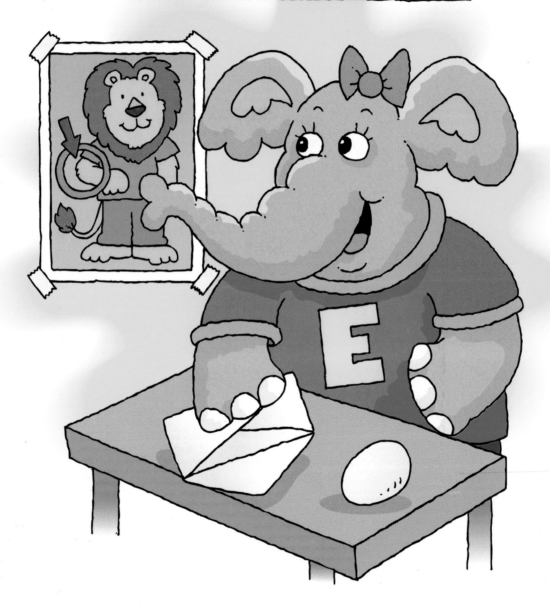

I am E.